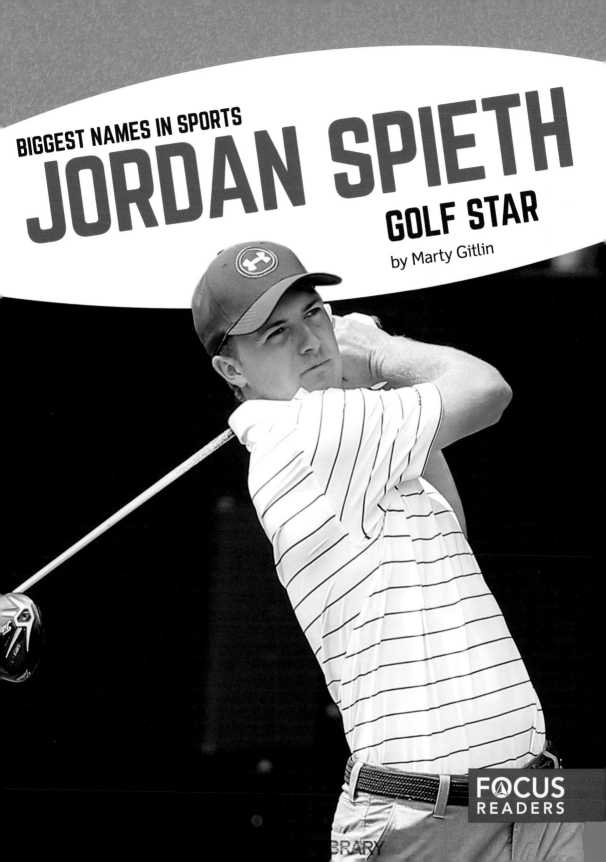

JORDAN SPIETH

GOLF STAR

by Marty Gitlin

FOCUS READERS

North Star
EDITIONS

WWW.NORTHSTAREDITIONS.COM

Produced for North Star Editions by Red Line Editorial.

Photographs ©: Rich Graessle/AP Images, cover, 1; Brian Murphy/Icon Sportswire/AP Images, 4–5; George Holland/Cal Sport Media/AP Images, 7; Ted S. Warren/AP Images, 8; Tony Gutierrez/AP Images, 10–11; Seth Poppel/Yearbook Library, 13; Jeff Roberson/AP Images, 14; Reed Saxon/ AP Images, 16–17; Eric Gay/AP Images, 19; Matt York/AP Images, 20; Todd Mizener/The Dispatch/AP Images, 22–23; Jon Super/AP Images, 25; Chris Carlson/AP Images, 26; Red Line Editorial, 29

ISBN
978-1-63517-045-0 (hardcover)
978-1-63517-101-3 (paperback)
978-1-63517-203-4 (ebook pdf)
978-1-63517-153-2 (hosted ebook)

J
92
Spieth,
Jordan

Library of Congress Control Number: 2016951015

Printed in the United States of America
Mankato, MN
November, 2016

ABOUT THE AUTHOR
Marty Gitlin is a sportswriter and educational book author based in Cleveland, Ohio. He has had more than 100 books published.

TABLE OF CONTENTS

CHAPTER 1

WINNING THE OPEN

Jordan Spieth had a long **birdie putt** in front of him. His ball rested 26 feet (7.9 m) from the cup. Many golfers would have been happy to putt twice and settle for **par**. But Spieth is not just any golfer. And he was on a roll. It was the final day of the 2015 US Open near Seattle, Washington.

Jordan Spieth launches a tee shot during the first round of the 2015 US Open.

Spieth was two **strokes** ahead of the field heading to the 16th hole. Now he needed an amazing shot to increase that lead. He eyed his target and looked at his putter. He glanced back at his target one more time. Then he tapped the ball gently. It curved slowly as it rolled toward the hole. Then the ball disappeared into the cup. Spieth hoisted his club into the air and pumped his fist. The crowd roared its approval.

Spieth was the hottest golfer in the world. Two months earlier, he had won the Masters. Another **major tournament** victory seemed to be in the bag. But his work was not done. Spieth smacked a

Spieth punches the ball out of the long grass on the 17th hole.

terrible shot into the thick, tall grass on the 17th hole. It led to a double **bogey** on the hole, dropping him back into a tie for the lead.

Spieth celebrates after winning the 2015 US Open.

Spieth had lost his lead but not his confidence. He rebounded to birdie the 18th hole. He then had to sweat it out as

Dustin Johnson attempted an **eagle** putt for the win. Johnson missed. Then he attempted a birdie putt to force a playoff the next day. He missed again. Spieth was the US Open champion.

At the age of 21, Spieth had become the youngest US Open winner since 1923. But the golf world was used to his heroics. He was already a mature golfer.

NOT JUST A KID

Spieth got used to being the center of attention in 2015. But he grew a little tired of those who seemed surprised that someone so young could achieve so much. He said he didn't feel like a rookie. He thought of all of the golfers on the tour as his peers.

CHAPTER 2

A GOLFER GROWS UP

Jordan Spieth was born and raised in Dallas, Texas. He seemed destined to be an athlete as a young child. Jordan's mom played basketball at Moravian College in Pennsylvania. His father was a baseball player at Lehigh University. Jordan's brother, Steven, was a standout basketball player at Brown University.

Jordan lines up a putt at the 2010 Byron Nelson Classic.

Jordan was a pitcher on his baseball team before his teenage years.

But when Jordan began to focus on golf, there was no stopping him. He had amazing talent and confidence. He stood out from the rest of the pack as a junior golfer.

Jordan often traveled to out-of-town events without his parents because they were busy taking care of his siblings. Jordan would share a hotel room with another player or stay with a host family. He had to learn to take care of himself. It forced him to grow up quickly.

It wasn't always easy. Jordan lost the Texas state high school championship

Jordan started playing golf at a very young age.

as a freshman after being penalized two strokes. The punishment was the result of a shouting match with fellow golfer and future University of Texas teammate Alex Moon.

Jordan played in the 2010 St. Jude Classic when he was just 16 years old.

But Jordan learned from his mistake. He kept his temper in check and won the Texas high school championship in each of the next three years.

Jordan's talent enabled him to compete beyond the high school level. At age 16, he played with the best in the world in the 2010 Byron Nelson Classic. He became the sixth-youngest golfer ever to make the **cut** in a Professional Golfers Association (PGA) Tour event. And even bigger things were just around the corner.

PIANO MAN

Jordan participated in more than just sports during his childhood. He and brother, Steven, also played the piano. According to their father, Jordan loved it, but Steven hated it. Jordan played well enough to be entered in local competitions. That fueled his fire. He loved to compete at anything.

CHAPTER 3

TERRIFIC AT TEXAS

The University of Texas golf team went 40 years without a national title. Jordan Spieth made sure the drought would not reach 41 years. He arrived in Austin, Texas, as a freshman in 2012. He immediately led the Longhorns to the national championship. He played a key role in the finals victory over Alabama.

Spieth (front row, center) and his Texas teammates celebrate their 2012 national championship.

Spieth was named Big 12 Conference Player of the Year as a sophomore. He was a first-team All-American. He was a finalist for the 2012 Ben Hogan Award, which is presented to the top **amateur** golfer in the country. He reached No. 1 in the World Amateur Golf Rankings. He had won two US Junior titles. The only other player ever to do that was the legendary Tiger Woods.

Spieth had already played in eight PGA events, and he had made the cut in five of them. Spieth tied for 21st at the 2012 US Open. That was the best finish among all of the amateurs in the tournament.

Spieth holds the medal he won for posting the lowest score by an amateur at the 2012 US Open.

Spieth poses for a photo with his family: father Shawn, mother Mary Christine, sister Ellie, and girlfriend Annie.

Spieth had nothing left to prove at the college level. He decided to leave Texas and join the PGA Tour.

As his golf prospects soared, Spieth stayed grounded in his personal life.

He continued to date Annie Verret, his high school sweetheart. He proved that fame and fortune would not change him. He enjoyed staying home and hanging out with his friends and family.

Spieth wanted to concentrate on golf. That dedication soon made him the best in the world. He also yearned to help those less fortunate. He achieved that as well. But the best was yet to come.

GIVING BACK

The Jordan Spieth Family Foundation supports special-needs youth, junior golfers, and military families. Spieth's sister, Ellie, has special needs and has been a source of inspiration during his career.

CHAPTER 4

CATCHING FIRE

Shortly after Jordan Spieth turned pro, his career faced a series of highs and lows. He missed the cut in four of his first 13 events in 2013. He placed 50th or lower in three others. But he also finished in the top 10 in four of those tournaments. Then, Spieth caught fire in July.

Spieth is fired up after chipping in from the bunker to force a playoff at the 2013 John Deere Classic.

He appeared to have no chance of winning the John Deere Classic in Silvis, Illinois. But Spieth sank six birdies on the last nine holes to force a playoff against Zach Johnson and David Hearn. It took five dramatic holes for Spieth to clinch the victory. The 19-year-old had become the youngest winner of a PGA Tour event in 82 years.

That victory earned him a spot in the British Open, which was played later that week in Scotland. Following the playoff, Spieth hopped on a plane and flew across the Atlantic Ocean. The whirlwind week ended with a top-50 finish for Spieth at the famed Muirfield golf course.

Spieth hits a tee shot on the 17th hole at Muirfield golf course during the 2013 British Open.

Amazingly, Spieth was still a week shy of his 20th birthday. Spieth finished the year with three top-five finishes and helped the United States win the Presidents Cup.

Spieth talks with US vice-captain Tiger Woods during the 2016 Ryder Cup.

Spieth struggled to match that form in 2014. His best showing was a second-place finish at the Masters. But he had one of the greatest seasons in golf history in 2015. Spieth finished in the top four in five of his first nine tournaments. He won two of them. Then he won the famed Masters Tournament in Augusta, Georgia. He also won the US Open in June.

Spieth placed in the top four in all four major tournaments in 2015. He finished the year ranked No. 1 in the world. In 2016 Spieth won two more tournaments before helping the United States pull out a thrilling victory over Europe in the Ryder Cup. Spieth and his fans looked forward to many more wins in the future.

JORDAN SPIETH

- Height: 6 feet 1 inch (185 cm)
- Weight: 185 pounds (84 kg)
- Birth date: July 27, 1993
- Birthplace: Dallas, Texas
- High school: Jesuit College Preparatory School
- College: University of Texas, Austin, Texas (2011–2013)
- Major tournament victories: Masters, Augusta, Georgia (2015); US Open, Seattle, Washington (2015)

Seattle

Dallas

Augusta

Austin

FOCUS ON
JORDAN SPIETH

Write your answers on a separate piece of paper.

1. Summarize Chapter 4 of this book.

2. When he was in high school, Jordan lost a tournament because he yelled at an opponent. Do you think that was a fair punishment? Why or why not?

3. Whom did Spieth beat in a playoff at the 2013 John Deere Classic?

    A. Alex Moon and Justin Thomas
    B. Zach Johnson and David Hearn
    C. Dustin Johnson and Tiger Woods

4. Why were people surprised that Spieth was winning so many tournaments in 2013?

    A. He hadn't been a very good golfer before then.
    B. He had a terrible attitude on the course.
    C. He was much younger than the rest of the players.

Answer key on page 32.

GLOSSARY

amateur
Someone who is not paid to perform an activity.

birdie
A score of one under par on a golf hole.

bogey
A score of one over par on a golf hole.

cut
When the number of players is reduced in a tournament, leaving only the players with the best scores to play the final rounds.

eagle
A score of two under par on a golf hole.

major tournament
The biggest annual tournaments in golf: the Masters, the US Open, the British Open, and the PGA Championship.

par
The score a good golfer should make on a hole.

putt
A shot on the green in which the golfer intends to roll the ball into the hole.

strokes
Golf shots.

TO LEARN MORE

BOOKS

Goldsworthy, Steve. *Golf.* New York: Weigl, 2014.

Howell, Brian. *The Masters.* Minneapolis: Abdo Publishing, 2013.

Siemens, Jared (ed.). *Golf Legends.* New York: Weigl, 2016.

NOTE TO EDUCATORS

Visit **www.focusreaders.com** to find lesson plans, activities, links, and other resources related to this title.

INDEX

Answer Key: 1. Answers will vary; **2.** Answers will vary; **3.** B; **4.** C